The haunted Caxton Gibbet Inn in Caxton, Cambridgeshire, in which the son of a former landlord murdered three guests and threw their bodies into a well at the foot of the staircase. Phantom footsteps have been heard on the stairs.

HAUNTED INNS AND TAVERNS

Andrew Green

Shire Publications Ltd

CONTENTS

Published in 1995 by Shire Publications Ltd, Cromwell House, Church Street, Princes Risborough, Buckinghamshire HP27 9AA, UK. Copyright © 1995 by Andrew Green. First published 1995. Shire Album 319. ISBN 0 7478 0294 7.

Andrew Green is hereby identified as the author of this work in accordance with Section 77 of the Copyright, Designs and Patents Act 1988.

Printed in Great Britain by CIT Printing Services, Press Buildings, Merlins Bridge, Haverfordwest, Dyfed SA61 1XF.

British Library Cataloguing in Publication Data: Green, Andrew. Haunted Inns and Taverns. – (Shire Albums; No. 319). I. Title. II. Series. 133.122. ISBN 0-7478-0294-7.

Reports of genuine ghosts and hauntings would be welcomed by the author or they can be sent to the Society for Psychical Research, 49 Marloes Road, London W8 6LA.

ACKNOWLEDGEMENTS

Acknowledgements for help and assistance are due to: the *Bedfordshire Times*, Colin Harmer of Mountfield, Paul Harris of Folkestone, Barry King of Dagenham Psychic Research Group, *Isle of Wight County Press*, Robin Laurence of Thanet Psychic Research Group, Sally McCabe of the former Bayeux Restaurant, Len Moakes of the Nottingham Psychic Research Society, Tony Ortzen formerly of Psychic Press, Joyce Pain of Battle, Tom Perrott, chairman of the Ghost Club, Guy Lyon Playfair, Jack Pleasant, John Rotheroe of Shire Publications, and above all my wife Norah, for her patience and great and continued encouragement.

The cover photograph is by David Ross. Other photographs are acknowledged as follows: Keith Dobney, page 22; Jacqueline Fearn, pages 10 and 25 (top); Andrew Green, pages 3, 4 (both), 5 (bottom), 11 (top left), 24 (bottom), 29, 32; Tom Perrott, page 27; Pilgrim International (photograph by Luned James), page 11 (centre left). All others are by Cadbury Lamb.

Cover: *The phantom of a sad lady in a white gown haunts the 'Vicar's Room' in the George Hotel, Dorchester-on-Thames, Oxfordshire. She remains unidentified and her background is unknown.*

The haunted Seven Stars Inn at Robertsbridge, East Sussex, has since 1971 suffered constant poltergeist activity associated with a legendary red monk, although a cowled figure in a light fawn habit was seen in 1970.

A VARIETY OF HAUNTINGS

There are few people who would disclaim the possible existence of ghosts, whatever they may be – spirits, visible examples of former lives or images in some form of electromagnetic energy. Perhaps because of the increasing amount of testimony in the form of statements from reliable witnesses, together with photographic, electronic and sometimes evidence captured by a video camera, some ten million people in the United Kingdom freely admit to having experienced some 'psychic' incident or manifestation.

Surveys indicate that the ten thousand allegedly haunted sites in Britain include a large percentage of the estimated sixty thousand hostelries in the country, many of which are affected in some way by phantoms of various kinds.

In general it seems difficult to reproduce the genial atmosphere of a typical British pub, though a number of attempts have been made and copies can be found in Europe, America and even the Far East. A few have reproduced the ambience so successfully that ghostly manifestations, such as might be associated with a genuine article, have occurred there.

The *Raffles Hotel* in Singapore, for example, is haunted by the ghostly sound of a young child singing 'Mary had a little lamb'. So well established is this unusual haunting that for safety reasons the manager had to ban the burning of joss sticks and the offering of incense to appease the disturbed spirit.

Another ghostly incident, probably associated with the English but in the United States, was reported in 1993. It affected the *Battery Carriage House Inn* in Charleston, South Carolina. A visiting engineer from North Carolina suddenly

Since Norman times the Shirley family have owned the estate on which the haunted Ettington Park Hotel, Stratford-upon-Avon, Warwickshire, stands. The ghosts include the appearance of a woman who committed suicide by hanging herself.

The Lion Hotel, Nyetimber, West Sussex, contains the ghost of 'a tall lady in dark grey or blue' who walks through the upstairs corridors.

The White Hart Hotel in the centre of Okehampton in Devon is the home of a ghostly young boy called Peter who keeps 'moving things around'.

In the Battle of Waterloo at Brighton, East Sussex, the landlord has felt 'a presence', but some customers have actually seen the phantom of a tall man in an old coachman's cloak.

woke one night to see the outline of 'a big man, broad and barrel-chested, wearing several layers of clothing, standing beside the bed. I managed to let out a bit of a squeal and the ghost vanished.' On investigation it was learnt that pirates used to be brought to the inn and hanged from a tree 'on the Battery'. 'This convinced me that the phantom I saw was that of an old pirate hanged centuries ago.'

Ballygalley Castle Hotel in County Antrim is a reminder of the extensive migration of Scots to Northern Ireland in the sixteenth and seventeenth centuries. The castle was built in 1625 by James Shaw, originally of Greenock in Scotland, but it was enlarged in Victorian times and even a former dungeon has now been converted into a lounge bar to enhance the atmosphere. One of the three ghosts that reside here may well be that of Lady Shaw, who, because of the heartless attitude of her husband, committed suicide by jumping from a tower window. Her footsteps have been heard crossing the bar and a member of the staff is convinced that he saw her. The sound of a rustling dress passing along a corridor and the inexplicable knocking on a certain bedroom door have, however, been associated with the invisible ghost of a Madame Nixon, but a guest who complained about the noise coming from the affected room saw the door slowly open to reveal a group of people wearing seventeenth-century costume. They were all miming as if enjoying a silent party, but the guest was later assured that there was no one there, let alone a group staying in that room.

Emphasising the number of cases of hauntings associated with former religious sites is the incident in 1978 experienced in the *Royal Hotel* in Cupar, Fife, Scotland. One of the assistant managers, on passing the functions room, noticed a light had been left on and, approaching the open doorway, saw a tall hooded figure, resembling that of a monk, glide across the room. On reaching the far wall the figure vanished and the light went out. Some weeks later a regular guest at the hotel witnessed an identical incident, even noticing that the door handle was 'freezing'.

The chief librarian of the region in offering an explanation pointed out that the hotel was constructed on the burial ground of St Catherine's Abbey.

Wales has also been affected by English attitudes and imposed culture, and one instance of this could well be that which affects the *Llangoed Hall Hotel* in Anglesey. Accepted by most witnesses as the antics of the ghost of Denzil Christie, a fourteen-year-old boy, is the havoc frequently found in the kitchen, where furniture is constantly rearranged by unseen hands. The lad has been seen both in the library and in room 1 of the hotel. Although the reason for his untimely death was given officially as a 'hunting accident', a local historian firmly believes Denzil was so appalled by the prospect of having to return to Eton that he shot himself.

It is a well-established fact, confirmed by an examination of any collection of hauntings, that few provide evidence of any injury to witnesses. The concept of ghosts can often make some people a little apprehensive but genuine apparitions can never actually harm anyone, even though they may, as has been claimed at the *Five Ways Inn* in Worcester, be seen to throw things, in this case a brass model aeroplane at a witness.

Some believe that ghosts can continue to exist for centuries and remain as visible examples of former lives only if witnessed by a person whose mind is 'in neutral' at the time. This idea can account for the majority of ghosts, both of the dead and of the living.

A case of the latter occurred at the *Ancient Briton* pub in Mile End, London, in 1975. Jim Marling was putting a crate of beer into the lift and turned to see the figure of a short blonde lady, wearing glasses and with her arms folded, looking intently at him. 'But she just faded away after a couple of seconds.' Jim made some enquiries about the 'ghost', only to discover that she was Florrie Clark, the former landlady, who was living quite happily some miles away in Goodmayes, Essex. 'It's funny to be a ghost', she said, 'but I must admit that I often picture myself being back in the old pub, watching Fred in the cellar putting another crate in the lift.'

It was in the 1980s that the manager of the *Beehive* in Coinage Hall Street, Helston, Cornwall, confirmed that his pub was haunted. When a local folk singer, who had been hired for the evening, went upstairs, he saw the figure of an old lady sitting in a rocking chair. He turned to ask a member of the staff what the unknown visitor was doing there but, on hearing a crash, turned to find that both the old lady and the chair had vanished, and not down the stairs.

The most convincing evidence of the other haunting at the pub is the number of visitors who have actually seen the ghost of a thirty-year-old man, 'always in shadow and after ten at night'. Locals believe that he is one of the victims of two murders that occurred in the pub some 150 years ago, but the problem with this idea is that the figure appears in 'modern-style clothing', so maybe it is another case of a living ghost ?

Another London pub, the *Horns* in Crucifix Lane, SE1, used to suffer so severely from the sound of a young girl, thought to be Mary Isaac, crying for her mother, that Canon Pearce-Higgins was called upon in 1979 to exorcise the ghost. This he did successfully, but the phantom of an unknown old woman still continues to 'glide about', though causing no trouble.

The Oak Room in the Weston Manor Hotel, Weston-on-the-Green, Oxfordshire, is where guests are likely to feel the presence of Maude, a nun burnt at the stake for her illicit love affair with a monk.

Right: *Jamaica Inn at Bolventor, Cornwall, was made famous by Daphne du Maurier's novel and houses the ghost of a sailor 'in a long old-fashioned coat and a three-cornered hat'.*

Below: *The Little Angel, Remenham, Berkshire, where the ghost of Mary Blandy, a young woman who murdered her father, is still witnessed.*

Below: *Thought to be ghosts of martyrs burnt at the stake are the two cloaked phantoms witnessed in the Chequers Inn in Amersham, Buckinghamshire.*

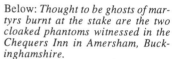

Left: *The Cowick Barton Inn, Exeter, Devon, houses the ghost of a cowled monk, probably from the nearby monastery of St Thomas, and he is advertised on one of the windows.*

Above: *Local legend has it that a victim of a naval press gang was killed in the White Hart Hotel in Hemel Hempstead, Hertfordshire, and his shouts and feelings of 'abject terror' can still be experienced.*

Above: *An incredible haunting by an unseen bird occurs at the King's Arms in Monkton Farleigh, Wiltshire, but footsteps are also heard sounding on non-existent stone flooring.*

Objects move inexplicably in the Talacre Arms, Holywell, Clwyd, and lamps light themselves without any power.

The licensee is often asked about the ghostly lady in the large hat who frequents the Cardinal's Error in Tonbridge, Kent, but her identity remains unknown.

A GHOST CAUGHT ON VIDEO AND AN UNFROCKED VICAR

An unusual case of a ghost appearing on a video is that in the old *Duke of Wellington* pub in Neath, West Glamorgan, where a number of weird 'disturbances' have occurred. Alarms and lights go off for no reason, mysterious bangs and crashes are heard and a feeling of being watched by an invisible presence is experienced. On one occasion a barmaid noticed 'a tall man disappear through the closed front door', but the highlight of the haunting was obtaining a record of the 'ghost' on the security video in July 1993. The tape clearly shows the back door swinging open by itself and then the misty figure of a tall man appears to glide swiftly across the picture until he moves out of range. No rational explanation has been forthcoming.

A more conventional haunting affected a London pub associated with Jack the Ripper, the renowned *Old Bull and Bush* in North End Road, Hampstead. In 1985 some rusting surgical knives and a skeleton wearing remnants of clothing were discovered

in a bricked-up cellar in the building. It was thought that it was part of a tunnel under a house owned by a surgeon who practised in the Whitechapel area, but for many years prior to the discovery customers and staff had been puzzled by the ghost of a 'Victorian-looking gentleman' seen crouched on a stool in the saloon bar.

Another unusual mystery surrounds the *Union* pub in Rye, East Sussex. The building seems to be haunted by the ghost of a young unmarried mother who was killed when she fell down the cellar steps, but the previous tenant of the fifteenth-century building had often heard the sound of someone walking along an empty corridor upstairs. During 1992 the new owner saw the ghost of a seventeen-year-old girl walk through the kitchen area and learnt that several members of his staff had also witnessed the phantom as well as sensing her presence. During a visit by researchers in 1993, sounds of banging were heard, 'laser-like flashes' were seen and the bar

The 'curse of the mummified cat' haunts the Mill Hotel in Sudbury, Suffolk (above). Every time the remains (below) are moved from its grave in the foyer 'there has been untold trouble'.

Right: A former licensee took out an insurance policy against any ill effects that might be suffered by customers who see any of the ghosts that haunt the King and Queen pub in Highworth, Wiltshire. The main spectre is of a hunchback monk.

Right: The Wicked Lady in St Albans, Hertfordshire, is a reminder of the notorious highwaywoman Lady Ferrars, but the haunting consists of the sound of a woman weeping, perhaps the widow of a victim.

door to the kitchen opened and closed by itself. A few days later a medium described the ghost of a tall man in 'what could be a naval uniform or perhaps that of a customs officer', a description that matched that of a figure seen a few days earlier.

The title of 'the oldest haunted inn' continues to be the subject of speculation and debate. One of the many claims is that made by another tavern in Rye, the *Mermaid*, which was reopened in 1420 to replace an earlier building which had been offering hospitality since 1300. The haunting was first experienced when the building was a private club. A guest awoke early one morning to see two men in doublets and hose fighting a silent duel, a fight thought to be between a member of the notorious Hawkhurst Gang of smugglers and a customs officer. Another ghost here is that of a seventeenth-century maid, thought to have been killed by her smuggler lover and his gang after she found out too much about their illegal activities.

An even older pub, the *Trip to Jerusalem* in Castle Rock, Nottingham, is stated to have been built in 1189 to provide refreshment to Crusaders before they began their journey to the Holy Land. The main ghostly incident occurred one October evening during the Second World War when a group of American soldiers were leaving to return to their billets and heard a woman's voice shouting from an empty room: *'Bel fitz, eiez pitie de gentil Mortimer.'* The mystified servicemen learnt later that in October 1330 Roger Mortimer, Earl of March, had committed a ghastly murder and taken up residence with the king's mother. The king, Edward III, accompanied by a group of soldiers, burst into his mother's room and despite her pleadings to 'have pity on the gentle Mortimer', seized the Earl and dragged him to the Tower of London, where he was found guilty of killing the king's father. He was taken to Tyburn, where he was hanged, drawn and quartered.

One of the most ancient London taverns is *Ye Olde Gate House* in Highgate West Hill, for its first licence was issued in 1310. The poor old lady ghost in a black dress who is occasionally witnessed in the rear part of the premises has been named as 'Mother Marnes', a widow and former owner who was murdered for her money when drovers used to bring their cattle up to Smithfield market in London. But she never appears when children are in the pub.

'An old man with a short white beard and a battered hat who seems to be searching for something' is the description given of the ghostly figure haunting the two-hundred-year-old *Blue Ball* in Oldbury, West Midlands. The licensee is one of a number of witnesses to the mysterious old ghost but, like many owners of haunted properties, they consider their unknown guest to be 'one of the family', though wishing they knew what he was looking for. He wears eighteenth-century clothing so cannot be associated with the bundle of ten shilling notes discovered under a loose brick in the cellars some years ago. The only disturb-

The Trip to Jerusalem, Nottingham, where American soldiers heard the ghostly voice of a medieval queen.

Left: *The ghost of an old lady haunts the Red Lion in Horndean, Hampshire, and some witnesses have experienced a weird desire to fall or jump from a specific window.*

Below: *Thought to be over 450 years old, the Green Dragon in Waltham Abbey, Essex, retains the ghost of a cavalier who visits the inn only at lunchtime.*

Above: *The haunting by a cavalier wearing a red cloak of the Gate Inn in Sutton Coldfield, West Midlands, was investigated and confirmed by a local research group in 1975.*

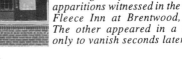

Left: *A ghostly monk is one of two apparitions witnessed in the Golden Fleece Inn at Brentwood, Essex. The other appeared in a mirror, only to vanish seconds later.*

ing aspect is that occasionally the old man has been seen peering into the tenant's bedroom and several times simply walking through a wall in the public bar.

The ghost of a Dutch cavalry officer has frequently been seen in the fourteenth-century pub called the *Dun Cow* in Abbey Foregate, Shrewsbury, Shropshire. This rather unusual phantom is accounted for by the report that one of Prince Rupert's stewards was murdered here by a Dutch army officer, who was hanged for the crime in the stables. Another weird phantom, witnessed in the same pub by the landlord and his wife, is that which appears to be a monk wearing a habit of very coarse material but 'covered in thousands of different-coloured dots'.

It is most unusual for poltergeist activity to last more than a few months unless there is constant stress being suffered by someone associated with the affected site. The *Mill Inn* at Withington, Gloucestershire, is one such building, where wine bottles and a number of kitchen utensils have been thrown around, but in 1990 the sighting of three ghosts was added to the haunting record. An old woman wearing a wide-brimmed hat with a veil covering her features was seen sitting by the fireside with 'misty figures of two men standing behind her'. 'The trio looked like some old faded photograph', said one witness, who suggested that the woman might be the former landlady who was drowned in the nearby river Coln.

The haunting by the ghost of an unfrocked vicar must be unique, but that is what occurs in the *Old Stocks Hotel* in Stow-on-the-Wold, Gloucestershire. A resident staying in room 17 in 1989 woke to see the figure of an elderly vicar leaning over her and, from the description she gave of the apparition 'before it faded away', it was possible to identify it as that of the Reverend Alan Burr, who, it seems, also plays an invisible piano occasionally.

As the majority of ghosts remain anonymous, affectionate nicknames are provided to give them some form of status or acceptability. One such is 'Bunty', the phantom of an unknown serving wench seen on at least three occasions since 1974 in the *Beehive* pub in Bath, Avon. The favourite places for her appearance are the hallway, 'where she just stands for a second or two before vanishing', and in one of the bedrooms.

Some of the mysteries surrounding haunted sites can also be caused by conflicting stories or are just simple tales created to amuse or frighten children. There are, for example, a number of explanations for the ghost at the *George Hotel* in Wallingford, Oxfordshire, but all relate to the sighting of 'a sad woman' in room 3, better known as the 'Tear Drop Room', in which one wall is covered in plasterwork resembling tear or pear drops. The popular idea is that the apparition is that of a suicide who, on learning of the sudden death of her lover in a fight, mixed soot with her tears and plastered the wall 'with her sorrowful misery', before hanging herself in the bedroom. In addition to the unhappy ghost, two phantom children standing by a handbasin in one of the rooms have also been reported. One wonders if they are related to the suicide.

The George Hotel, Wallingford, where a ghost described as a 'sad woman' haunts the Tear Drop Room.

Left: *Not only have inexplicable footsteps been heard in the George, Chertsey, Surrey, but an 'invisible something' has been known to sit on beds.*

Left: *The Other Tap and Spile, originally the Yorkshire Hussar, in North Street, York, is haunted by a 'black figure with a cape on its shoulder'.*

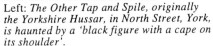

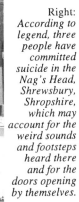

Right: *According to legend, three people have committed suicide in the Nag's Head, Shrewsbury, Shropshire, which may account for the weird sounds and footsteps heard there and for the doors opening by themselves.*

Left: *One of the smallest pubs in England, the Nutshell in Bury St Edmunds, Suffolk, contains the ghost of a small boy murdered here many years ago but still occasionally seen in a bedroom.*

15

One of the most haunted pubs in Suffolk, the Crown Inn, Bildeston, has four ghosts: a lady who hanged herself, an old man who sits in the lounge and two children in Victorian clothing who walk silently through the lounge.

PHANTOM CATS AND DOGS
AND LADIES IN RED

In the small Cumbrian village of Brough, which sits astride the Swindale Beck, is the *Traveller's Rest*, the residence of a ghostly woman in a long black gown holding a large bunch of keys. Some believe that she is associated in some way with the nearby castle; she was last seen in November 1985 by a visitor from overseas.

South of Washington, in Tyne and Wear, in the hamlet of Fatfield is the popular eighteenth-century *Havelock Arms*, where the unusual figure of a 'man over six feet tall wearing a green silk threaded waistcoat' was seen by a young guest in one of the bedrooms. The deputy manager of the inn confirmed the description matched that of the ghostly 'Long John', once a regular and popular customer always seen in a green waistcoat.

A few years ago the author had argued the case for ghosts on a BBC radio programme and a couple of days later was contacted by the former barman of the *Old Talbot* in Worcester, to confirm de-

tails of the haunting there. On starting work, he was told that a particular area was haunted by a phantom cat, which was frequently observed rushing through the bar. Two weeks later, whilst tidying up the bar, he noticed that the hotel Dalmatian had jumped to its feet, was snarling and trembling with its hackles raised menacingly and together they 'watched' something invisible pass by. Shortly afterwards, both the manager and the barman not only saw 'a grey cat-like creature' rush past and vanish at one of the locked doors but, he said, 'I actually felt it brush against my trouser leg'.

Is the ghost of a man who hanged himself in the cellars of the *Radclyffe Arms* in Oldham, Lancashire, during Edwardian times still haunting the tavern? The landlord and his wife have heard so many reports of his appearance that they have named the pipe-smoking phantom 'Ernie'. He has also been witnessed by their daughter, who, early one morning, went into the bar, 'spoke to someone and then came to

The Castle Hotel in Conwy, Gwynedd, suffers from various unusual manifestations, including whistling noises and a ghostly cat.

tell us that there was a customer wanting to be served, but there was no one there'.

There have been a number of visitors to the *Birdcage Inn* at Thame in Oxfordshire who have experienced the inexplicable haunting of this old tavern. One noteworthy incident was when two cameramen, who were helping to make a film in the town, reported having seen 'a sort of cold mist' drifting out of their bedroom door and hearing unidentifiable footsteps on the landing at 2 o'clock in the morning. The men had opened the door but found nothing to account for the noise, nor for the mysterious movement of the till whenever the haunting was discussed.

The phantom voices of an angry couple having an 'unholy quarrel' affect the *Naval and Military Inn* at East Reach in Taunton, Somerset. A former landlord felt that the atmosphere created by the verbal threats and horrendous abuse from the unseen pair was 'really evil'. 'It was so bad that we had to close up the bedroom',

he told members of a psychic research group. Three other young visitors, fishermen down for the weekend, 'were so scared of the atmosphere in the room that they came down in the middle of the night to sleep on the floor'.

An even more unusual haunting occurs in the *Lower Angel* in Warrington, Cheshire, for here, according to the landlord, barmaids suffer what could be termed as 'sexual harassment of the basic level'. A number of female members of the staff, on bending down, have felt someone or something 'give their bottom a playful tweak'. At first they were extremely annoyed and upset but, on realising that no humans were anywhere near them at the time, they have come to accept that the ghost of Dick Peabody is responsible. He was notorious in the nineteenth century for taking delight in caressing 'full and rounded buttocks'. He was also known as a 'bed swerver' – someone unfaithful to his wife. The current landlord feels that no real harm is being suffered and he

The medieval doorway of the Tudor Rose Hotel in King's Lynn, Norfolk, where the ghost of a 'small woman in grey' is seen both by visitors and by members of the staff.

The Llandoger Trow in Bristol once held the ghost of a sailor dragging one leg. Now all that is reported is the sound of a limping man.

woman just turned away and returned upstairs without responding. A few seconds later he went upstairs to find that his mother had not moved from her seat in the saloon bar, but he learnt that 'a presence' had also been felt in the bathroom.

Even more disturbing are the effects of the ghostly visitations in the *Bell Inn* in Bell Road, Hounslow, Middlesex, for here beer kegs are actually smashed and taps left running, despite the double locks on the cellar doors, and the ghost of a tall man 'who looks like a highwayman' is occasionally sighted. A gibbet used to stand opposite the pub, displaying the rotting corpses of such 'gentlemen of the road'.

Only a few yards away, on the Staines Road, another pub, the *Hussars*, is similarly affected by another highwayman, for such a figure has been seen striding through the corridors towards the cellars. Here mysterious shadows have been noted by members of the staff, who have also

prefers to wait and see what, if anything, develops.

At the *Crown Inn*, Alton, Hampshire, a scratching noise has often been heard issuing from the chimney breast in the dining room. At first it was thought to be caused by a rat or an unfortunate bird that had fallen from the roof, but the sound of whimpering and scratching has been persistent over the years. Locals believe that the phenomenon results from a dog that was killed by its master in a drunken rage, beating it to death against the chimney. Strength was added to this legend when in 1967 workmen renovating the dining room found the skeleton of a dog that had obviously been very badly treated.

One morning in 1991 the new landlords of the *Black Boy* pub in Upper Halling, Kent, found the bar covered in water and discovered that the glass-washing machine had turned itself on during the night and was flooding. On another occasion the landlord was working in the cellar and, hearing someone on the stairway behind him, turned to see the figure of a woman in red. Because he thought it was his mother he asked what she wanted, but the

The Bell Inn, Hounslow. Here beer kegs have been inexplicably smashed and taps left running despite locked doors.

18

The figure of a woman wearing a fitted cardigan was assumed to be that of a customer at Ye Olde Leathern Bottel in Northfleet, Kent, until she suddenly vanished, but another phantom is that of a tall fair-headed man.

discovered locked doors opening and closing on their own and curtains thrown open after being closed for the night.

The tenant of the *Bridge Inn*, Stapleton, North Yorkshire, was so concerned with the incidents in his pub in 1993 that he was considering calling for an exorcism. The ghostly footsteps continue but of greater concern are the facts that gas cookers have been switching themselves on even when the pub has been closed and doors linked to a sophisticated security system have been found unlocked.

Alveston Manor at Clapton Bridge in Warwickshire, now a hotel, was formerly a Tudor manor house. Shakespeare's first open-air performance of *A Midsummer Night's Dream* took place at the manor, which stands on a former Saxon burial ground. The ghost that haunts the place, however, is that of neither a Saxon warrior nor of the Bard, but that of a little girl who died alone during 'a grand party' held during the early twentieth century.

A room in the Bull Hotel, Wargrave, Berkshire, is where some visitors hear the sound of a woman crying and they feel 'desperately sad'.

The well-known Bull Hotel in Long Melford, Suffolk, contains 'psychic mysteries' such as objects moving across the room by themselves.

Her sad little figure is sometimes sitting at the bottom of the four-poster bed in the room in which she was discovered, but how she died has never been established. What puzzled a journalist who hoped to see the ghost was being woken by the sound of a man in an upper room talking very loudly. On enquiring as to who was staying in the room, she was assured that there was no room above her bedroom and, what is more, none next to it.

The White Hart, Minster Lovell, Oxfordshire, houses a ghostly, silently weeping woman, probably Rosalind, who committed suicide here during the Victorian era.

Right: *Known internationally for the ghost of a Guards officer who was caught cheating at cards and later killed, the Grenadier, in Wilton Row, Belgravia, London SW1, has been the site of constant investigation by scientists and researchers.*

Above left: *Hopcroft's Holt near Steeple Aston, Oxfordshire, is where a landlord and his wife were murdered. It is thought that this accounts for the ghostly figure of a 'middle-aged man' being seen in one of the bedrooms.*

Cracking noises, bluish lights which vanish 'into a wardrobe' and sounds of an explosion have all been experienced in the Queen's Head, Blyford, Suffolk.

The figure of a ghostly monk is seen and his presence felt in the Brocket Arms, Ayot St Lawrence, Hertfordshire, towards the end of the year. That was the season when he was hanged from a ceiling beam, in the reign of Henry VIII.

DICK WHITTINGTON AND AN ARMY OFFICER

In the sixteenth century an apprehensive Emperor of Austria tried to ensure that no ghosts disturbed his sleep when staying in taverns or hotels in his travels around Europe by calling on his troops to visit the establishments on his itinerary well before his arrival.

Whether Bill Clinton, the President of the United States, tried to arrange the same procedure prior to his visit to Aylesbury, Buckinghamshire, in 1994 is not known, but no doubt the White House security team kept an eye open for any phantoms. What is clear is that the apparition of John Lee, the former owner of *Hartwell House*, where he died in 1866 before it became a hotel, did not appear during the President's stay. Nevertheless he has been seen several times sitting quietly in the library there and sometimes strolling in the garden. Part of the cellars incorporate a tunnel that once led to a nearby monastery and it is from this area that sounds of clinking glasses and mumbled singing are heard, created, it is thought, by ghostly monks.

The *Bear* at Chippenham in Wiltshire

is haunted by rather an unusual type of ghost, but one might wonder if there is such a thing as a usual phantom. When a maid, on her way to start work in the pub, glanced up at a bedroom window, she noticed that it was open and a lady in grey was pulling back the curtain. But a few minutes later, when she went to tidy up, she realised that the window was closed and learnt that no one had stayed there that night, though a barman had reported hearing loud noises from another empty room at the same time. The manager wondered whether the 'lady in grey' could be the ghost of a canoness from Lacock Abbey, before it was dissolved in 1539, for the nun's clothing was described as being 'of a coarse grey cloth'.

The *Capricorn Club* on the Military Road at Brighstone, Isle of Wight, replaced a roadhouse built in 1972 on the site of a former officers' billet that had been destroyed in the Second World War by a bomb which killed ten men. In one part of the tavern there have been several instances of customers suddenly feeling 'overpowered with sadness' and of being aware of 'an unknown figure'. 'He looks like an Army officer', said one witness.

The newly appointed manager of the *King's Arms*, in St Mary's Street, Bedford, told the author in November 1994 that there was no doubt that his pub was haunted. 'My cellarman has seen him [the ghost] once as a youngish man in a short-sleeved shirt and a friend has also heard the footsteps in the same locality.' There could well be a connection between these incidents and the fact that the building was originally a monastery and then a morgue.

A few years ago a respected research group spent three days investigating the ghostly happenings at the *Golden Lion Hotel* in St Ives, Cambridgeshire. The belief is that the ghost of Oliver Cromwell

The Golden Lion, St Ives, Cambridgeshire. The phantom Green Lady seen here is said to have been Cromwell's mistress.

haunts the place because it was his headquarters, but the phantom more often described is that of 'Ivy', the Green Lady. Her portrait hangs in the restaurant and is thought to be that of Cromwell's mistress, who acted as a nursemaid to his children before she eventually hanged herself in room 14.

A ghostly lady in white resides in the *Castle Hotel* in Castleton, Derbyshire. She is veiled, being the phantom of a jilted bride who committed suicide as a result of being left in the lurch at the church. She is also associated with the apparition of a youngish man 'in a pinstripe suit' who is occasionally seen with her.

Ghosts seldom die away completely unless aided and, despite attempts to dispense with the hauntings in the *Crown Hotel* in Market Street, Poole, Dorset, phenomena continue. One day in 1975 the milkman told the licensee that he was getting upset by the sound of children screaming and the wife of the landlord agreed, having also heard the distressing disturbance. Since then more ghostly happenings have been experienced, including the sound of a piano being played and, even less enchanting, the 'sound of something heavy, like a body, being dragged across a floor' in a room above the stable block. Locals believe that a previous landlord killed his two deformed children after imprisoning them for months in the stables.

One day in 1750 Betty Radcliffe, owner of the *Bell Hotel* in King Street, Thetford, Norfolk, died, either by committing suicide by jumping from a balcony outside room 12, or by being murdered by her lover and thrown from the gallery. Whatever the cause of her death, the sound of her distressing cries and sobs has often been reported by guests staying in an adjoining room, and on occasions her ghost has been witnessed walking slowly along a nearby corridor, 'wringing her

In the Belper Arms, Newton Burgoland, Leicestershire, a number of visitors have complained about a feeling of being suffocated in one particular bedroom.

hands in a state of anguish and utter misery'.

Who better to haunt the *Whittington Inn* in Kinver, Staffordshire, than Dick Whittington himself, the former owner, or even Lady Jane Grey, who lived there as a child? Figures of both are claimed to

have been seen over the years but more substantial has been the testimony of a former waiter at the tavern, who provided a signed statement concerning his vivid and unpleasant experience in a particular bedroom, though he was not the only sufferer. The incident, which all agreed was

The Golden Grove, Chertsey, Surrey, is haunted by the ghost of a young girl found murdered in one of the bedrooms and thought to have been killed by a local monk.

The 150-year-old George Hotel in Lydd, Kent, is haunted by a phantom cat that jumps on beds. It was seen in 1978 by a young boy staying the night.

the Duke of Monmouth's officers were billeted before the battle of Sedgemoor. On occasions, the sound of a violin being played has been heard but the musician has been seen only once, one Christmas Eve, when she appeared in 'a beautiful gown of a seventeenth-century design' before gently fading away.

Not far from the famous Aintree race-course, near Kirkby in Merseyside, lies *Melling Hall Hotel*, which has at least two active ghosts. One of these is that of Lady Darlington, who owned the building during the early twentieth century. She has been observed near one of the main stair-ways. Also seen is the phantom of a small, but nevertheless ghostly, dog complete with name tag hanging from its collar.

Originally a hostel for the Knights Templar, but later used by King John as a court house, the *Angel and Royal Hotel* in Grantham is now a delightful centre for visitors to Lincolnshire. A building with such a history might be expected to be full

'certainly no nightmare', consisted of a feel-ing of 'an inexplicable pressure on both legs and my neck', whilst the atmosphere in the room seriously affected a dog, for it was obvious that some invisible force was holding him down on the floor.

Considered by some to be well estab-lished is the ghost of Dorothy Forster, which is stated to haunt the *Lord Crewe Arms* in Blanchland on the borders of Dur-ham and Northumberland. The more tan-gible haunting is that of a weird knocking accompanied by 'a weird sensation' and, for three guests, feeling 'a thump at the bottom of the bed', all occurring in the Bamburgh Room. In another room a fig-ure of a monk has been seen and is as-sumed to be a former resident of the ab-bot's guest house, which was on the site up to the sixteenth century.

Practically every trade and profession is represented by ghosts, though violin-ists seem to be few and far between. One case that has been recorded is at the *Castle Hotel*, in Taunton, Somerset. The hotel was once part of the castle, where

The Castle Hotel, Taunton, where a ghostly violinist has occasionally been heard, but only once seen.

The Royal Oak, East Lavant, West Sussex, accommodates the phantom of a 'thin bearded man'. He is thought to be a long dead relative of a former licensee.

'A sort of bluish light' and weird inexplicable sounds are the main hauntings at the Plough, Clifton Hampden, Oxfordshire, but also doors mysteriously open by themselves.

The Boar's Head, Bishop's Stortford, Hertfordshire, is one of the three taverns visited by the ghost of the 'Grey Lady', who vanishes outside St Michael's church.

of shades of the past, but the only haunting here is that of an unknown lady in a white gown who glides, rather sedately, through the second- and third-floor corridors. There has been the occasional report of a certain bedroom being afflicted with a shaking bed, 'but it only shudders for about half a minute', according to one victim.

A Devon pub that reported an interesting haunting in 1994 was the *Smugglers' Haunt Hotel* in Brixham, where staff have seen the reflection of a man at an empty table when they glance in a mirror, a guest had his bedclothes removed during the night and a porter saw the figure of a man in his bedroom, which vanished on being told to 'buzz off'. The phantom was dressed in eighteenth-century costume.

One of the best-known ghosts in England is Sukie, a maid who was killed in a scuffle with members of the Hell Fire Club. She continues to be witnessed in the George and Dragon in West Wycombe, Buckinghamshire.

WHY INNS AND TAVERNS?

That hauntings have been fully accepted since olden times is highlighted by the case of Athenodorus, an ancient Greek who, whilst staying in a small tavern some two thousand years ago, found himself unable to sleep until he had investigated the sudden appearance of a ghostly slave who had directed him to his own burial site. The authenticity of the manacled spectre was confirmed by the finding of a chained skeleton in a grave at the precise spot indicated by the apparition.

The age of a building seldom has any relevance to a genuine haunting, although an old house will have seen more life and death than a recently constructed property. To emphasise the value of some of the ancient taverns in the United Kingdom, the British government issued guidelines in October 1994 for the preservation of pubs, but how these can be attuned to ghosts remains to be seen.

The small selection of cases described in this book includes an instance of a modern building affected by comparatively recent deaths – the *Capricorn Club* in the Isle of Wight – whilst some others suggest that renovation or modernisation of the premises has been the catalyst to generate some paranormal phenomenon; physical disturbance has created a 'haunting'.

But wherever people congregate, even for short periods, there is always a risk of tragedy, be it murder, suicide or simply a sudden accident as in the *Angel*, Petworth, West Sussex. Some years ago two elderly ladies were staying at the inn and one evening the younger lady was waiting in the dining room for her friend to come down for dinner, but she never arrived. She had fallen when coming downstairs and was killed. On learning of the tragedy her companion had a heart attack and died, but her ghost continues to wait near the inglenook.

Some experts think that it is this type of incident that creates a 'ghost'. The shock of learning of the unforeseen death seems

The apparition of 'Old Bill', an ancient farmworker, often appears in a bedroom in the Elvey Farm Hotel, Pluckley, Kent. He used to walk around and on two occasions threw a saddle on the floor.

to create a mental image of the victim – an apparition. Many of the buildings mentioned in this book stand on sites where tragedy has occurred or, in even more cases, an appalling incident of unexpected death occurred within their walls.

Nevertheless pubs and taverns are the natural place for a family gathering, entertainment or simply a quiet drink with friends. It was Dr Samuel Johnson who asserted that 'there is nothing which has yet been contrived by man by which so much happiness is produced as by a good tavern or inn'. And where better to enjoy the pleasure of home-like comforts than 'a good tavern or inn' – especially one that is haunted?

FURTHER READING

Brooks, John. *Good Ghost Guide*. Jarrold, 1994.

Byrne, Linda. 'A Ghost called Florrie', *Barking and Dagenham Post*, 3rd December 1975.

Coysh, A.W. *Historic English Inns*. David & Charles, 1972.

Cutting, Angela. *Leicestershire Ghost Stories*. Anderson, Blaby, 1990.

Donkling, Leslie, and Wright, Gordon. *Dictionary of Pub Names*. Routledge & Kegan Paul, 1987.

Evans, Hilary. *Visions, Apparitions, Alien Visitors*. Aquarian Press, 1984.

Fairclough, Charles. *Chester Ghosts and Poltergeists*. Fairclough, undated.

Forman, Joan. *Haunted East Anglia*. Robert Hale, 1974.

Forman, Joan. *Haunted South*. Robert Hale, 1978.

Gauld, Alan, and Cornell, A.D. *Poltergeists*. Routledge & Kegan Paul, 1979.

Green, Andrew. *Our Haunted Kingdom*. Wolfe, 1972.

Green, Andrew. *Ghost Hunting, A Practical Guide*. Garnstone, 1973.

Green, Andrew. *Phantom Ladies*. Bailey Bros & Swinfen, 1977.

Green, Andrew. *Ghosts of Today*. Kaye & Ward, 1980.

Green, Andrew. *Haunted Houses*. Shire, reprinted 1994.

Hallam, Jack. *Haunted Inns of England*. Wolfe, 1972.

Hapgood, Sarah. *500 British Ghosts and Hauntings*. Foulsham, 1993.

Harris, Paul. *Ghosts of Shepway*. Harris, 1994.

Hippisley Coxe, A. *Haunted Britain*. Hutchinson, 1973.

Hirth, Eric. *Ghosts in Cornwall*. St Ives, 1986.

Mackenzie, Andrew. *Hauntings and Apparitions*. Heinemann, 1982.

McCarthy, Christine. *Ghostly Tales of Shropshire*. Shropshire Libraries, 1988.

Mead, Robin. *Weekend Haunts*. Impact Books, 1994.

Metcalfe, Leon. *Discovering Ghosts*. Shire, second edition, 1994.

Moakes, Len. *Haunted Nottinghamshire* (volume 2). J.H. Hall, Derby, 1993.

Playfair, Guy Lyon. *Haunted Pub Guide*. Harrap, 1985.

Royal, Margaret, and Girvan, Ian. *Local Ghosts*. Abson Books, 1976.

Smith, Charles. *In Praise of Pubs*. Reader's Digest, 1987.

Topping, Richard. 'Cheers', *Leisure Time Magazine*, volume 1, number 3. Zonecraft, 1989.

Turner, Mark. *Folklore and Mysteries of the Cotswolds*. Hale, 1993.

Walsh, Alexandra. 'Haunted London' in 'Aspects', *Ealing Recorder*, 29th October 1993.

Whitaker, Terence. *Ghosts of England*. Hale, 1987.

Wilson, Colin. *Poltergeists*. New English Library, 1981.

Wilson, Colin, and Odell, Robin. *Jack the Ripper*. Bantam Press, 1987.

Wiltshire, Kathleen. *Ghosts and Legends of the Wiltshire Countryside*. Compton Russell, 1973.

INDEX OF INNS AND TAVERNS

Gloucestershire 14
Old Talbot, Worcester, Worcestershire 16
Other Tap and Spile, York, North York-
shire 15
Plough, Clifton Hampden, Oxfordshire 26
Queen's Head, Blyford, Suffolk 21
Radclyffe Arms, Oldham, Lancashire 16
Raffles Hotel, Singapore 3
Red Lion, Horndean, Hampshire 13
Royal Hotel, Cupar, Fife 6
Royal Oak, East Lavant, West Sussex 26
Seven Stars, Robertsbridge, East Sussex 3
Smuggler's Haunt Hotel, Brixham, Devon 27
Talacre Arms, Holywell, Clwyd 9
Traveller's Rest, Brough, Cumbria 16
Trip to Jerusalem, Nottingham, Notting-
hamshire 12
Tudor Rose Hotel, King's Lynn, Norfolk 17
Union, Rye, East Sussex 10
Weston Manor Hotel, Weston-on-the-
Green, Oxfordshire 7
White Hart Hotel, Hemel Hempstead, Hertfordshire 9
White Hart Hotel, Minster Lovell, Oxfordshire 20
White Hart Hotel, Okehampton, Devon 5
Whittington Inn, Kinver, Staffordshire 24
Wicked Lady, St Albans, Hertfordshire 11
Ye Olde Gate House, Highgate, London 12
Ye Olde Leathern Bottel, Northfleet, Kent 19

A number of guests staying in room 1 of the Angel Hotel in Guildford, Surrey, have seen the ghost of what appears to be a Polish army officer in a First World War uniform.